The Tr...

De bat...

WITHDRAWN

The crisis
surrounding
gender identity

WITHDRAWN

Stephen Whittle

SOUTH
Street PRESS

The Transgender Debate
The crisis surrounding gender identity

South Street Press is an imprint of
Garnet Publishing Limited

Published by
Garnet Publishing Limited
8 Southern Court
South Street
Reading
RG1 4QS
UK

ISBN 1 902932 16 1

First Edition 2000

British Library Cataloguing-in-Publication
Data. A catalogue record for this book is
available from the British Library.

House editor: Louise Gallagher
Jacket and book design: Michael Hinks
Printed in Lebanon

N 305.9066
A43ГЛ4

Contents

Introduction

'Trans' has become a cultural obsession in recent years. Television, film and the news media all seek out new angles and story lines that include people who have 'changed sex'. In our daily lives we cannot escape being reminded that there are now many people in our society who have undergone this drastic life-changing process. Popular images include Hayley in *Coronation Street* and Dil in Neil Jordan's successful film *The Crying Game*. And of course the true-life transsexual woman Dana International who won the Eurovision Song Contest for Israel in 1998.

In summer 1999 television viewers were once again watching another instalment in the twenty-year real life saga of a transsexual woman in *George to Julia*. The staff room at work was buzzing as fellow workers asked me such questions as, 'Are things any better now?', 'There can't be many doctors like that now, can there?', 'Do people still want to change sex?' and so on.

Trying to answer such questions is very hard because over the past 25 years since I 'changed sex' the situation for the trans community has changed so much. The techniques of gender reassignment surgery have made great leaps and bounds, yet trans people still face all sorts of problems. Issues such as rationing within the National Health Service here in the United Kingdom have reared their ugly heads, and transsexual people have invariably found their needs placed at the bottom of the list. All over the world we have seen many transsexual people seeking legal recognition of their new 'sex' through courts and parliaments. Transsexual people can now serve in many of the armies of the world – though it is still rare that they do. We see them publicly in a way that was unthinkable 25 years ago, when the only way to survive as a transsexual person was to be as secretive as possible about one's past role in life. Now rarely a month goes by without another newspaper report about someone seeking equal rights in court, and rarely a week goes by without another feature appearing in a women's magazine. The range of stories being told is vast: the headmaster who became the headmistress, the surgeon whose title changed from Mr to Miss, the lorry driver who used to be a ladies' aerobic teacher.

Yet despite all this media interest and the vast amounts of information available on the Internet, many people still do not know what it means when their co-worker says 'I'm transsexual and I'm starting gender reassignment treatment'. Even less is understood when a teenage daughter tells her parents that she is going to have hormone treatment in order to live her life as the gay man she feels she is. One might argue that it is astonishing that ignorance about trans lives can still exist after the media deluge. In fact, such lack of knowledge is not surprising at all. Gender identity is such an inherent and fundamental part of all our lives that those whose gender identity coincides with their sexed body cannot possibly understand how anyone might wish to change it. And there lies the crux of the issue – the trans person, whether transsexual, transgender or transvestite, is not seeking to change his or her gender identity at all. What trans people are trying to do is find a way of presenting their gender identity in such a way that the rest of the world will understand who they are.

Understanding
Gender

The term gender was initially used just to refer to the linguistic associations between the two sexes, for example the pronouns 'he' and 'she'. In the 1940s and 1950s those involved in the study of sexual behaviour and activity used the term to refer to those behaviours that were more associated with men (male gender roles and behaviours) and women (female gender roles and behaviours). Since the 1960s and the rise of feminism, it has come to have a more complex relationship with the world we live in and we now use the word to refer to the social organization of the relationship between the sexes. Gender is about social relations that are determined through social and cultural choices, but it is also much more than that.

Gender is very different from sex – sex roles and gender roles used to be interchangeable terms but increasingly we maintain a distinction between biological (sex) and social (gender) relations. Nevertheless it is often very hard to maintain the distinction; sex and gender (and we have not even included the biological categories) are still quite jumbled up. It is one thing to say someone has a vulva, vagina, clitoris, breasts, ovaries, etc, it is quite another thing to assume that person is either female, feminine or a woman. Sex is in fact a very complex biological concept which is rarely as unambiguous as we think, as we shall see later when we look at intersexuality and what it tells us about the sex of people. Gender, unlike the apparently straightforward sex categories, has several aspects: gender assignment, role, identity and attribution.

Man/Woman: Humanoid in that they are language-dependent categories which arrive with self-perception and which bring about a sense of personal individuality with group sameness that can be communicated through language.

Masculine/Feminine: Descriptive terms for social and cultural language of the self, socially controlling but can also be empowering for the individual in confirming the branch of humanity to which they belong. Also relates to the individual's ability to play their gendered social role well. Used by some to refer to the socially constructed categories we live in.

Male/Female Gender: A social construction, not just about individuals and their adoption of social roles, but also about how gendered relations are perpetuated through organizational practices as well as social and cultural practices. Used by some to refer to the biologically determined categories we live in.

Gender identity

Gender identity is the total perception of an individual about his or her own gender. It includes a basic personal identity as a boy or girl, man or woman, as well as personal judgements about the individual's level of conformity to the societal norms of masculinity and femininity. Gender as it is perceived by others is called gender role. The two concepts are tied together, since most people show their perceptions of themselves in their dress, manners and activities. Clothing is the major symbol of gender that allows other people to identify the individual's gender role immediately, but there are other symbols as well, including mannerisms, gait and occupational choice. For most people their gender identity, gender role, and all the symbolic manifestations of gender will be congruent, and they will be sexually attracted to the opposite sex. People who are transvestite, transsexual or transgender may feel they do not fit neatly into either the male or female role or their behaviour is not totally congruent with the rules and expectations of the society they live in.

Theories of gender development

It is not possible at the present time to point to a specific gene related to gender identity, but it is possible to infer a genetic influence from current secondary research data. There are three main theories as to how gender identity develops: biological development, socialization and a mix of both.

Firstly, studies of syndromes such as Klinefelter's or Turner's which result out of abnormalities of sex chromosomes show that chromosomes have long been known to influence gender identity. However, the details of the genetic process as it relates to masculinity and femininity are still being researched. There is evidence that multifaceted genetic and hormonal factors have other, more subtle, effects. There is a vast and growing scientific literature documenting hormonal influence on perceived gender behaviour. Animal studies have shown the impact of prenatal environments, particularly the sex hormonal status, on the developing structure of the brain and the development of masculine or feminine gender roles.

Gender assignment: answers the question: 'What do the authorities say I am?' In most cultures it's the male or female designation. It is a category decided by a doctor at birth, usually after a cursory visual inspection to determine the presence (male) or absence (female) of a penis. Generally cultures assign some permanent, immutable gender at birth. A few societies do allow people to change their gender assignment later in life. Gender assignment is something that is done to each one of us, long before we have any ability to have any say in the matter.

Gender role: answers the question: 'What does the culture think I should do with my life?' It's the sum total of qualities, mannerisms, duties and cultural expectations accorded a specific gender as assigned.

Gender identity: answers the question: 'Am I a man or a woman or something else entirely?' Most people don't think about this one very much. They let gender assignment stand in for gender identity. But identity is personal; it's what we feel our gender to be at any given moment. This feeling may be influenced by biological factors that have a cultural tag sticking out of each one of them.

Gender attribution: is what we all do when we meet someone: we decide whether they're a man or a woman, or something indeterminable. We attribute a gender based on an intricate system of cues, varying from culture to culture. The cues can range from physical appearance and mannerisms to context, and the use of power.

Adapted from *My Gender Workbook* by K. Bornstein, London, Routledge, 1998

Sex hormones are the messengers that cause bodily reactions which are interpreted as male or female. Their influence is not limited to the post-natal development of a person but may be equally or even more important in the prenatal period. There is now evidence to show that gender identity is related to the structure of the brain itself. A recent study from the Netherlands looked at the region of the hypothalamus, the bed nucleus of the stria terminalis (BST), which is smaller in women than in men. Remarkably, the region was of female size or smaller in the brains of the six male to female transsexual women studied. The Dutch study also showed that in the brains of transsexual women, the hypothalamus BST was within the size range of a female brain, and not a male's. The study was also able to show that it was highly unlikely that this size difference was a result of any hormone treatment they had undergone, as the hypothalamus BST develops fully whilst the foetus is in the womb.

Secondly, there is the socialization theory which postulates that certain children are born with a gender identity that leans to the other side of the gender continuum to varying degrees. Children are not born with a specific identity as transvestite, transsexual or transgender – rather these patterns are shaped by social and environmental factors.

It is no longer possible to argue that either nature or nurture alone is the answer; it is clear that both are involved in producing the complex person we call a man or a woman. The physical distinction between men and women is not absolute, as individuals are now scientifically regarded as living on a continuum, with female characteristics at one extreme and male ones at the other.

Gender identity is the result of a complex interaction amongst three factors:

- a genetic predisposition,
- physiological factors,
- the socialization process.

Research continues to seek the causality of gender identity, and cross-gender identity in particular. There are no definite answers about the source of gender identity or sexual orientation, but our understanding is growing. Professor John Money has stated that:

> causality with respect to gender identity disorder is sub-divisible into genetic, prenatal hormonal, post-natal social, and post-pubertal hormonal determinants … there is no one cause of a gender role … Nature is not responsible, nor is nurture, alone … They work together, hand in glove.

'The concept of gender identity disorder in childhood and adolescence after 39 years' by J. Money in *Journal of Sex and Marital Therapy*, 20(3), 1994, pp. 163–77

Understanding Trans

Clarifying some matters

As our understanding of sex and gender becomes more complex, so does our understanding of ourselves. Most people shelve these complexities as they move beyond puberty and instead concentrate on the problems of getting a job, paying the bills and keeping a home. But for a not inconsiderable number of people, those who are in some way trans, the complexities cannot be shelved and have to be faced. This is not only because their lives are unfulfilled, if not miserable, if they fail to do so, but also because they are labelled by society in derogatory terms: queer, tranny, dyke, etc. Those terms will dictate whether or not they are going to be allowed to have a job, whether they will be able to enjoy their home in peace and in safety, whether or not they are going to be able to give their significant others the same support and protection that other families are afforded by the state.

Recently we have seen a massive 'coming out' of the trans community, and an adoption of a community identity through the acquisition and the empowerment of new labels and new meanings. Which of these labels people adopt for themselves very much depends upon how they 'know' their own gender identity, and how the rest of the world understands those labels. Let's start by looking at the labels and what they mean to those people to whom they matter: trans people (at the back of this book you will find a glossary including many other relevant terms).

Transsexuality

Transsexual people have a gender identity – their sense of maleness or femaleness – which differs from their anatomical sex. This clash of sex and gender is medically termed gender dysphoria and it will cause a person so much emotional pain that he/she must ultimately deal with this issue – generally by seeking gender reassignment.

The term 'transsexual' first appeared in 1949 in the phrase 'transexualis psychopathia' which was coined by David Cauldwell, a writer of popular newspaper medical columns, to describe someone we would probably now recognize as being transsexual. It first appeared in the medical literature in 1954 in a paper written by Harry Benjamin, a doctor specializing in hormone therapies, and a counsellor, physician and supporter of many transsexual people.
'Transsexualism and Transvestism as Psycho-somatic and Somato-psychic Syndromes' by H. Benjamin in *American Journal of Psychotherapy*, 8: 219-230, 1954

Difficulties lie with the semantic understanding of the word 'transsexual'. Simplistically, as an adjective derived from the Latin, it means crossing (*trans*) from one sex to the other. But that makes certain a priori assumptions: that we know what sex is, and that we know what 'crossing over' is. The word has come to embody the populist view of the 'sex change case' – some idea that people choose to change sex and are provided with sex reassignment surgery (SRS); they start off as one sex and become another.

In 1953, she was a scandal

When George Jorgensen decided to change his name – and his body – the nation wasn't quite ready

By Michele Ingrassia

Newsday, May 5, 1989, Friday, ALL EDITIONS

IT WAS meant to be a private affair, a quiet series of operations that would change the 26-year-old Bronx photographer into a woman and, in the process, exorcise the personal demons that had haunted him since childhood. But even before she left the Copenhagen hospital in February, 1953 – transformed from George Jorgensen Jr., the 98-pound ex-GI, into Christine Jorgensen, 'the convertible blonde' – word had leaked out. Overnight, it became the most shocking, most celebrated surgery of the century. And even if the furore eventually waned, the curiosity lingered, following Jorgensen to her death on Wednesday at San Clemente General Hospital after a 2½-year battle with bladder and lung cancer. She was 62.

'I could never understand why I was receiving so much attention,' Jorgensen said in a 1986 interview. 'Now, looking back, I realize it was the beginning of the Sexual Revolution, and I just happened to be one of the trigger mechanisms.'

As early as 1967, in his foreword to an autobiography by the transsexual woman Christine Jorgensen, the endocrinologist Harry Benjamin, who pioneered research into transsexualism, was casting doubt on the idea that transsexual people underwent sex reassignment treatment; rather, forecasting a view that would be upheld by many transsexual people today, that they sought out gender confirmation treatment.

The endocrinologist Harry Benjamin said that he first attempted to induce breast growth in a male patient by means of female hormones in the 1920s.

Dr Gohrbandt, Director of the Surgical Clinic of the Urban Hospital in Berlin, is believed to have performed the first modern, complete male to female gender reassignment surgery in 1931. Also in 1931, Dr Felix Abraham, who worked at the Institute for Sexology in Berlin, Germany, published the first article on gender reassignment surgery, describing Dr Gohrbandt's surgery. ('Genital Reassignment of two male transvestites' by F. Abraham in *Zeitschrift fur sexualwissenschaft und sexual Politik*, 18: 223–6, 1937.)

The first biography of a transsexual woman was that of Danish painter Lili Elbe (formerly Einar Wegener) who underwent 'sex change' surgery in 1931 with Dr Gohrbandt. She died within a year of complications from the surgical procedures to form a new vagina. Her biography *Man into Woman* was published in 1937. (*Man into Woman* by N. Hayer in Essex, Anchor, 1937.)

He says of Christine (who transitioned to living as a woman in 1952, at the age of 26):

> But was this female gender role really new? The vivid description of her early life supplies a negative answer. This was a little girl, not a boy (in spite of the anatomy) who grew up in this remarkably sound and normal family.

A Personal Autobiography, by C. Jorgensen, New York, Eriksson Inc., 1967, p. vii

The word 'transsexual' is increasingly considered a misnomer, particularly by transsexual people themselves. For physicians it has become a signifier for those individuals who seek hormonal and surgical intervention to make them physically more like those people in the opposite sex group. Within the shorthand of the world of medicine it has become accepted that:

> The transsexual is genitally an anatomical male or female who expresses with strong conviction that he or she has the mind of the opposite sex, who lives as a member of the opposite sex part-time or full-time, and who seeks to change his or her sex legally and through hormonal and surgical sex reassignment.

Venuses Penuses, by J. Money, New York, Prometheus Books, 1986, p. 375

Transsexual people sometimes agree with the above view, but not always. They have also developed various other descriptions of their personal state to explain their own predicament. However 'transsexual' will be used herein for those people who actively seek, in one form or another, hormonal and surgical intervention to make their bodies resemble more closely that of the opposite anatomical sex group, and who choose to live in the gender role of that group if at all possible.

Transgender

Even with today's medical knowledge and available intervention techniques, there are people who identify themselves as transsexual but who choose for various reasons not to take all the steps that lead to hormonal and surgical reassignment. There are also people for whom such treatment does not seem the answer to their problem, albeit they choose to live considerable parts of their life in the opposite sex role. Furthermore, defining 'transsexual' is an extremely difficult task. Any definition has to accommodate more than one lifestyle. Cultural and historical changes regarding our knowledge of gender also alter our view of who would be known as transsexual, and who would self-identify as such. Accordingly, various descriptive phrases can be used to describe individuals who might fit into the modern-day category of transsexual.

Transgender was originally coined to be used as a term inclusive of all these people. There are many historical characters who 'cross-gender lived' for significant parts of their lives at a time when hormonal and surgical reassignment treatment was not yet developed. These people were often 'claimed' by the lesbian and gay communities as part of their own, but transsexual people felt that their history was being taken away. Certainly for a lot of these characters there is no evidence at all of their sexual preferences or practices; there is just evidence that they lived their lives as men or women in opposition to their anatomical sex, just as many people who do not undergo gender reassignment do nowadays.

In the 1990s transgender has become an umbrella term which covers many different types of people who are part of a unique community. The community is defined both by self-identification and by the oppression that its members suffer because of their gender identity or gender presentation. Individuals may identify as transgender because they cross-dress some of the time, because they cross-gender live much of the time, because they undergo gender reassignment, or just because their gender identity or gender role is not conventional. Furthermore, gender role oppression is not unique to transsexual people, although they are often the most visible victims of it. Many women also suffer from gender role oppression and many lesbian and gay people face homophobic attacks not because of who they sleep with but because they are seen as being butch or effeminate. Transgender is a very inclusive term; the transgender community is made up of those who choose to identify with it because their gender identity or gender role faces some sort of attack.

Transvestism

The public perception of transvestism is of men dressing up as nurses, French maids, schoolgirls in high heels or other erotic garb. Such 'transvestism' has little if anything to do with gender identity. Rather, it is a fetishistic practice that is role play, rather than gender role confusion, and for many it is associated with reaching sexual orgasm. However for many transvestite men, as they mature, cross-dressing becomes less associated with sexual relief than with a sense of personal well-being and relaxation. Transvestism is mostly a male activity but in fact there are many activities and clubs for women that have comparable clothing rituals. If, as many transvestite men say, it becomes a case of enjoying the sensation of wearing certain sorts of material and clothing, then the same could be said of some women's forms of pleasure. A 'drag queen' is not the same as a transvestite. Drag queens present caricatures of themselves as women rather than trying to emulate women.

Intersexuality

For most people the things that make up their sex and their gender identity are congruent.

XY chromosomes + testicles + penis + male identity
+ masculine role = man

XX chromosomes + ovaries + vagina + female identity
+ feminine role = woman

These things do not always coincide. When the physical attributes of chromosomes, gonads (testicles or ovaries) and genitals (penis or vagina) do not coincide in the manner we expect, then the individual has an intersex condition.

There are many intersex conditions now recognized by medicine and it is estimated that one in every 200 children is born with one. Some can be seen at birth but many are only ascertained later in life. For example, a teenage girl may not start her periods as expected and it will be discovered that she has 'Androgen Insensitivity Syndrome' (AIS). AIS women appear at birth to be girls and will grow up to become young women. They will have a vagina (often foreshortened but this will not be discovered until they start a sexual relationship), but in fact their gonads will be undeveloped testes hidden deep inside their bodies and they will have XY chromosomes. In many ways they could be said to be men, but, because their bodies were insensitive to the androgen that is produced in the womb when a baby has XY chromosomes, they failed to develop into boys. In effect these individuals have features of both sexes, yet for all practical purposes and by appearance and (generally) gender identity they are women, albeit infertile women.

Hermaphroditism is a very rare form of intersexuality in which the individual will have both sets of genital organs – a penis and a vagina. Interestingly, the law regards hermaphrodites as whichever sex they choose for themselves, but it does insist that once chosen, that sex is fixed for the remainder of life. Intersexuality and hermaphroditism are very different matters from trans. On occasions they overlap, and there is some relationship with some trans people. A person who is trans will have a masculine or feminine role which does not match up with the other factors in the above equations. It may well be that an intersexual syndrome affects an individual's perception of their own gender identity, but as said earlier, the formation of gender identity is a complex multifactorial issue, not exclusively dependent on either nature or nurture.

Sexuality and sexual orientation

None of the above – transsexuality, transgender or transvestism – has any direct relationship to sexuality. They are to do with gender identity, or in the case of transvestism, role-play. As in the general population sexual orientation is varied. Despite popular conceptions, people do not 'change sex' because they are ashamed or unable to adapt to a gay or lesbian sexual orientation. Gay men are attracted to men and would not desire a transsexual woman; similarly, lesbian women are attracted to other women and would not desire a transsexual man. Trans people generally undergo gender reassignment without changing their sexual orientation – transsexual people are just as likely to be straight, gay, lesbian or bisexual in their new gender role as any people are. However, although there is no relationship to sexuality, there may be an adaptation of sexual practice to accommodate the transsexual person's pre- or post-operative sexual organs. It may also be the case that many trans people are more flexible than the general population about matters of desire and sexual attractiveness, as they would be the first to admit that it is what is between the ears that makes a person, and not what is between the legs.

The mechanics of gender reassignment

Transsexual people will, without exception, say that they have always known that something was wrong. They will talk of an unhappy childhood and of having been aware that they should have been of the opposite sex. Some will talk of feeling that they are 'trapped in the wrong body'. Often a chance reading of a magazine article or watching of a television programme suddenly brings a realization that something can be done, i.e. a 'sex change', and that there is a name for how they feel.

Achieving gender reassignment is not easy. Despite the popular image, it is not a case of going into hospital one day as Joe and coming out the next day as Joanne. The process will take several years, involve several doctors and probably more than one operation. Even after someone has had the full surgery available to them (and not all people are able to have all the possible operations), the transsexual person will face a lifetime of supplemental hormone therapy and monitoring for possible side effects.

Most transsexual people first seek help from the family doctor, but typically family doctors will know very little as it is highly unlikely that they will have seen any other transsexual people in their clinical practice. There are only a very few specialist clinics throughout the world, but here in the UK generally the transsexual person will be referred to one of three main centres (in London, Leeds and Newcastle). Initially a psychiatrist at the specialist clinic will assess the patient and establish a diagnosis.

To be diagnosed as transsexual requires three criteria to be met:
- The desire to live and be accepted as a member of the opposite sex, usually accompanied by the wish to make his or her body as congruent as possible with the preferred sex through surgery and hormone treatment.
- The transsexual identity has been present persistently for at least two years.
- The disorder is not a symptom of a mental disorder or a chromosomal abnormality.

Generally a second opinion from another psychiatrist will be required to confirm the diagnosis.

Usually there will then be an opportunity for the patient to participate in an ongoing counselling programme, which may include family members. Often patients have suffered anxiety and depression owing to their isolation, and to the stress involved in clarifying the problem for themselves. Clinics often provide support through liaison psychiatric services to resolve these issues. When the diagnosis is confirmed, the difficulties of reassignment are explained and the patient is offered commencement of gender reassignment subject to their beginning what is known as the 'Real Life Experience' (RLE). Often the process may seem long and extremely hard to the person who is sure that gender reassignment is the solution to their problems, and it is often possible to bypass many stages of the procedure by seeking treatment in the private sector. But this is not risk free. Although some doctors will offer immediate hormone therapy or surgery, in some cases this may not be helpful as a period of psychological adjustment is essential to a person's future success in their new role.

RLE involves the patient living for one to two years in their desired gender role. They will legally change their name, and much of their documentation. They will start hormone therapy: testosterone for the female to male transsexual (FTM) and oestrogen for the male to female transsexual (MTF). Gradually over the next few months they will begin to experience changes in their body. It is almost as if they are going through puberty again, but in the opposite sex.

When an FTM person starts hormone therapy (from this point on I will refer to the female to male transsexual person as him/he/his as that is how he sees himself) his periods stop, he will experience a greatly increased sexual appetite, and he will notice a vast difference in his food intake. Over the next few months his voice will gradually break until it achieves a masculine tone, and by the end of the first year he may have enough facial hair to grow his first moustache. His waist will thicken, and he might (if he does some exercise) develop a fairly muscular body. Over several years of hormone therapy his clitoris will enlarge so that it begins to resemble a micro-penis. However, his breasts will not reduce in size, and the FTM will have to bind them using a purpose-made vest. About a year after he starts living in his new gender role he will undergo a bilateral mastectomy. This removes the breast tissue, reduces the nipple size and contours a masculine-looking chest wall. A hysterectomy is an option but many find it unnecessary after menstruation has ceased; it is however recommended when FTMs reach their early 50s as there is a slightly increased risk of developing cancer of the cervix.

Surgery to create a penis (phalloplasty) is very difficult. Though surgical techniques are improving, the surgery is not readily available, it is very expensive and it involves several surgical procedures. As a consequence most FTMs choose not to undergo it. More possible is a procedure called metoidioplasty whereby the hood of the clitoris is released and consequently it looks longer, though it may still not be suitable for penetrative intercourse. When supplemented with silicon implants into the labia to resemble testicles, the finished result can look like an ordinary small penis and testes. The urethra can be extended to the clitoral tip and so the FTM can urinate standing up. FTM gender reassignment treatment is generally very successful in terms of enabling the FTM to resemble a biological man, but the limitations of genital surgery will always mean that there will be circumstances in which he will have to disclose his past.

When an MTF person starts hormone therapy (from this point on I will refer to the male to female transsexual person as she/her as that is how she sees herself) her beard will soften, but it will not disappear. She will require electrolysis or laser treatment to remove it altogether. Her sexual appetite will reduce and she will find it more difficult to obtain an erection and reach orgasm. Her voice will not rise in pitch and the MTF may well need speech therapy to help her obtain a more female tone to her voice. Her body will change shape and become more feminine as she develops more subcutaneous fat. This will give her wider hips, and a less bony feel to her arms and legs. If she has suffered from baldness, she may find that she will have some hair regrowth, but it will rarely be sufficient to render some supplementary support such as a wig or a hair transplant unnecessary. She will have some breast growth, but it may not be adequate and she may later opt for silicon implants. One to three years after starting living in her new gender role she will undergo genital reassignment surgery. This involves an orchidectomy to remove the testes, and a penectomy to remove the core tissue of the penis. A hole in the position of the vagina will be created, and the new vagina will be lined with the surface skin that remains from the penis. The urethra will be shortened, producing a new opening next to the vagina, and nowadays a small section of the tip of the penis will be reconnected to the nerves and will become a new clitoris. The skin of the scrotal sac will then be sculpted to form labial lips for the new vagina. These surgical procedures are now, on the whole, very successful and after some time many doctors can not tell that the transsexual woman has had a surgically created vagina, although it will never self-lubricate in the manner of an ordinary vagina. Many transsexual women face the problem of an inherently male body structure, and for some it is often difficult for them to 'pass' well enough for nobody to know their past history. Some help can be given with supplementary surgical procedures such as nose and chin reduction, and the Adam's apple can even be shaved nowadays to reduce its prominence. However, for many the treatment is aesthetically very good, particularly if they start the route to reassignment young enough.

The prognosis for the transsexual person is now exceedingly good, hormone therapy and surgery having been greatly refined. There are still some long-term health risks being discovered as for the first time ever we see a cohort of people who have been living post-operatively in their new gender role for over twenty years. However, several follow-up studies have shown success rates of over 97 per cent when assessing elements such as friendship networks, social skills, personal sense of happiness and the feeling that the right decision was made. But not all is rosy; research on employment has shown that many risk losing their job or housing on transition, that their personal finances will suffer, and that they are at a greater risk of becoming a victim of harassment or assault. Like racism, sexism and homophobia, transphobia is also endemic in our society.

Facts and Figures

Numerically speaking?

The idea that there are very few transsexual people and that the condition is statistically insignificant, has permeated the literature surrounding the issue. The reality is that nobody knows how many individuals, either worldwide or in the United Kingdom alone, identify themselves as transsexual.

It might seem a comparatively simple job to count up those who attend specialist clinics that deal with the medical needs of transsexuals. This has been shown not to be the case. There has been a significant reticence on the part of hospitals and the health service as a whole to support gender reassignment work. Because of the social stigma surrounding the condition, clinics or medical teams receive little, if any, private or community support or funding for research. It remains the fact that in most of the world (including the United Kingdom) the care of transsexual people is essentially the concern of a few individuals who have chosen to specialize in this field. It is rare to find the sort of funded and committed multidisciplinary team that now exists at the Free University Hospital in Amsterdam.

Despite this scarcity of funding, a vast amount of research has been done with transsexual people, but this has come from individual practitioners who have pursued their own research interests and career development. However, generally figures are not available to show how many transsexual people have been treated or received gender reassignment surgery at the few specialist clinics or teams. Even if these were available, they would not include those people who have received sufficient treatment for their needs, from local medical practitioners, nor include those who have chosen to 'change over' without treatment.

The former 'Bond Girl' and transsexual woman, Caroline Cossey, in the foreword to her autobiography *My Story* writes:

'Transsexuals are in a minority. But it is a larger minority than many might imagine. To date many thousands of sex change operations have been performed in this country, and many more abroad.'

My Story by C. Cossey, London, Faber & Faber, 1991

Statistics at the Gender Identity Clinic of the Free University Hospital in Amsterdam are beginning to shed some light on the matter. In Holland, because it is possible legally to 'change sex' if an individual goes through the clinic programme, most people who wish to live full-time in their new gender role choose to participate in the clinic programme. The Amsterdam Gender Identity Clinic estimates that one in 11,900 men and one in 30,000 women will at least seek hormonal treatment in order to live in the gender role opposite to their anatomic sex. If these figures are extrapolated to the United Kingdom, we would expect there to be 2,265 (male to female) transsexual women, and 935 (female to male) transsexual men. This is obviously a gross underestimate when you consider that the major British campaigning group for trans rights, Press For Change, sends its newsletter out to over 2,000 people and it is highly unlikely that they reach even fifty per cent of their interested population group.

Liz Hodgkinson in her book *BodyShock* states that about one in 10,000 of the world's population are transsexual (making 5,500 in the United Kingdom) and that:

'Once considered an extremely rare and exotic occurrence, transsexualism now seems to be an almost everyday phenomenon. Though sensational "sex change" cases still make newspaper headlines, we have become quite used to them. At one time objects of pity, disgust or horrified fascination, known transsexuals now exist in almost every walk of life, as civil servants, entertainers, nurses, doctors, professional tennis players, artists, writers, computer consultants, university lecturers, teachers and housewives.'

Bodyshock: the truth about changing sex by L. Hodgkinson, London, Columbus, 1987.

There is little value in pulling these figures 'out of the hat', and even less in trying to prove one set or the other. But it is important to try to understand that the level of incidence is sufficient to mean that a large number of individuals, both nationally and worldwide, attempt and often succeed in obtaining some form of gender reassignment treatment. The numbers may be statistically insignificant as regards the political and cultural profile of many countries, but they have been sufficient in some states to persuade the legislative or judicial systems to accommodate the legal needs of transsexuals within them. Whichever figures are used, it is apparent that the prevalence rate of the transsexual condition is far greater than most people, including physicians, think.

'Worldwide, that "small number" (in their various forms) added up to between fifty and sixty million people – or the entire population of France.'
Statement by a delegate to the 1993 European Council Colloquy on Transsexualism, Medicine and the Law.

Geographically speaking?

Cross-gender living (as opposed to gender reassignment surgery) is certainly not an exclusive phenomenon of Western societies, nor of recent history. Transgendered behaviour is sometimes a fundamental aspect of homosexual subcultures or of transvestite eroticism in many societies, but it can also be completely unrelated to sexual behaviour. As non-sexual behaviour, that is, as a manifestation of gender identity, it can be used in varying degrees and with different meanings depending upon the modifications of the general culture in which it is placed. It can, for example, be associated with non-erotic transvestite activity such as the shaman priests of many pre-Christian religions, with the entertainment industry such as the lei dancers of Sydney, or with radical opposition to sex stereotypes as we sometimes see in the USA. Or, as in the case of transsexuals and other cross-gender people, it can be representative of a deeper desire on the part of the individual to be seen as a member of the opposite sex.

It has been argued that transsexualism is purely modern and that it did not come into existence until its definition in 1949. However, cross-gender living is not solely a modern occurrence in Western societies as there is evidence of cross-gender living, as a manifestation of gender variance, in many societies.

Martius wrote in 1867 of discovering in Brazil that:
'men are found dressed as women and solely occupying themselves with feminine occupations ... they are called cudinas, i.e. circumcised.'
Studies in the Psychology of Sex, vol. 1 by H. Ellis, London, Random House, 1948

Anthropologists first began to take note of cross-living behaviour amongst various peoples in the early part of the nineteenth century.

Waldemar Bogoras (in *The Spirit and the Flesh; Sexual Diversity in American Indian Culture* by W. L. Williams, Boston, Beacon Press, 1988) lived amongst the Chukchi of Siberia from 1890 to 1908. He describes seven gender categories – in addition to the categories woman and man – used by the Chukchi. Though individual Chukchi could choose to 'change sex' there were other genders which Chukchi could take up which did not involve a change from one sex

Oskar Baumann wrote in 1899:

'Among the negro population of Zanzibar ... male congenital inverts ... are attracted toward female occupations. As they grow older they wear women's clothes, dress their hair in women's fashion and behave altogether like women ... it is noteworthy that the natives make a clear distinction between them and men prostitutes. The latter are looked down on with contempt, while the former as being what they are "by the will of God" are tolerated.'

Studies in the Psychology of Sex, vol. 1 by H. Ellis, London, Random House, 1948

to another, but rather from one gender to another. Most noticeably they could choose not to stay in their original gender, but they did not necessarily become of the opposite gender as we understand it. One example is that of the yirka-la ul. S/he was anatomically male but would arrange his/her hair as if s/he was a woman, associate in the life of women in the tribe, and usually marry a man. The yirka-la ul was respected as a shaman for his/her healing and spiritual powers. The husband of a yirka-la ul would have high status amongst their people because of his marriage to a shaman, but in the home he would take a secondary role to the spirit husband of the yirka-la ul.

Similar categories were recognized in other groupings such as the Koryak and Kamchadel in Siberia. The practice was also found by Langsdorff (as mentioned in *Voyages and Travels*, 1814) to be common across the Bering Straits in Alaska amongst, among others, the Aleuts and the Kodiak Island Eskimos (Ellis, 1948).

A number of North American tribal Indian groups have recorded examples of cross-gender living, amongst which the institution of the Bedarche has been well documented. The North American concept of the Bedarche includes many different types of gender that existed in these native societies, but it is very difficult for those of us who live in a world of binary gender roles to fully grasp their meaning. However, in Western European modernist terms it could be said that Bedarches did include some transgendered individuals.

Similarly, in Polynesian societies there are records of the Mahu, Fa'a Fine and Wakawawine, who like the North Americans manifested a range of cross-living or transgendered behaviour. Also, amongst the various ethnic groups that inhabit Northern Albania and the Western Balkans there are still being reported cases of the 'sworn virgin'. The sworn virgin is an anatomical female who adopts the role, dress and behaviour of a man, and who is accorded the privileges and status which are afforded to men in their societies.

It must be noted that cross-gender living is not necessarily synonymous with a desire to 'change sex' but it is often closely related. It can be argued that if surgery and hormone treatment had been available to people who historically had led cross-gender lives, then they might have chosen to refer to themselves as transsexual, or if not that, at least use some of the facilities that are now available to transsexual people. Examples of groups who have done this are the Hijari of Northern India and the She-males of Singapore and Thailand. ('Male Transsexuals in Singapore' by B. H. Chia in *Singapore Medical Journal*, 22 pt 5, 280–3, 1981.)

The Hijari have for centuries practised the surgical art of castration and penectomy, a traditional skill. But, although they adopt the dress and mannerisms of women, they do not become women: they are Hijari, which is a distinct sex grouping. Recently, many have started to obtain and take female hormone therapy. This enables some of them to 'pass' well enough to be accepted as women by the community they live in. For many this is desirable, as being Hijari means facing limited tolerance and some scorn as they are an extremely low caste group. Many She-males in Singapore and Thailand now choose to use hormones and to have sex reassignment surgery. Traditionally their work has been as prostitutes and dancers, but hormones and surgery are for many of them a passport to a more conventional lifestyle.

The idea that transsexuality is purely a Western phenomenon fails to account for the desire on the part of many cross-gender people in other parts of the world to actually undergo sex reassignment. For many people throughout the world cross-gender living was, and often still is, a no-alternative solution to an otherwise unbearable problem.

Historically Speaking

An early history of transgender

In Western culture there is a long history of individuals who were transgendered. Ancient Greek and Roman writers commented on young men who desired to live their lives as women. The Roman goddess Venus Castina responded with sympathy and understanding to the yearnings of feminine souls locked in male bodies.

The influence of Christianity appears to have led to the first call for transgender behaviour to be punished, citing Deuteronomy 22:5 where there appears a prohibition of the wearing of male attire by women, or of female dress by men. The early medieval church included cross-dressing in the list of offences against God, or of heresies. However, there is a lot of evidence of the medieval and Renaissance male cross-dresser, particularly as street prostitute and actor. Both Church and secular law tended to deal with the breaking of sexual rules, rather than social mores. Throughout medieval Europe there was a belief that witches possessed potions that could change the sex of humans or animals. There was also a belief that demons could change others and

the Chevalier D'Eon de Beaumont's life (1728–1810) as a woman and as a French spy at the English Court has been written about many times.

Edward Hyde, Governor of New York and New Jersey (1701–8) and often regarded as the first known English transvestite, when he opened the New York legislature dressed as a woman, said:

'You are very stupid not to see the propriety of it. In this place and particularly on this occasion I represent a woman [Queen Anne] and ought in all respects to represent her as faithfully as I can.'

However, in the latter half of the seventeenth century we see evidence of a cross-dressing culture developing alongside the 'gay scene' in the taverns of London. These bars became known as molly houses ('molly' was originally a term for a female prostitute and, like the word 'queen', became a term for the effeminate male homosexual).

In the early 1800s the popular perception by the general public of any cross-dressing activity changed. From being a form of disguise or theatre it became the identifier of a certain sort of homosexual man. Although it did not persist as a pervading image of the homosexual, except in the style of the 'queen', the image of the molly gave rise to the concept of a distinctive homosexual culture and identity, and the development of a protective subculture for those involved.

Some mollies not only assumed female nicknames, or adopted feminine language, but created pregnancy rituals, culminating in mock lyings-in where a 'pregnant' man gave birth to a doll ... In short the mollies were ... playing out the other domestic roles of men and women.
Sex, Death and Punishment by R. Davenport-Hines, London, W. Collins and Son Ltd, 1990, pp. 72–3

The start of the scientific study of sexology

In 1885 the Criminal Law Act was passed in the UK which made all homosexual behaviour illegal and not just the sexual act. When this happened, those accused could face imprisonment and hard labour for up to two years. Those people who cross-dressed or cross-gender lived became easy targets of the law because they were associated in the public mind with the homosexual subculture. The 1885 Criminal Law Act became infamous as a 'blackmailers' charter'. As a result of this, people who were trans sought out doctors who could 'cure' them, diagnose them and help them to put aside their dangerous desires and aid them towards re-establishing their place in 'normal' society.

As homosexuals turned to the medical profession for cure, a whole new field in medicine developed: sexology. Doctors who worked with these patients were able to collect together many case studies. From these they discovered that rather than homosexuals being all the same, there was great diversity, both in individual history and also in practice and desire. This diversity was to allow the separation of transgendered people from other 'homosexual' patients.

One of the first public trials for transvestite behaviour was that of Ernest (Stella) Boulton and Fred (Fanny) Park. They were arrested in 1870 for indecent behaviour. Two cross-dressers, they were immediately examined for evidence of homosexual activity, and charged with conspiracy to commit such acts. They had frequented the haunts of female prostitutes for over two years, and the police were of the opinion that they were working as male prostitutes. The authorities lacked knowledge of the subject and based the prosecution on their transvestism and their soliciting of men as women rather than the act of sodomy. No conviction could be obtained on these grounds and they were ultimately acquitted of the charge of 'conspiracy to commit a felony by cross-dressing'. One of the biggest organizations for tranvestite men in the USA nowadays is the Boulton and Park Society.

The first sexologist who took a special interest in the sexual impulses of individuals was probably Richard von Krafft-Ebbing (1840–1902), Professor of Psychiatry at Vienna University. His *Psychopathia Sexualis* was published in constantly revised forms from 1877 to after his death. Krafft-Ebbing in this revision process constantly endeavoured to give clearer and clearer classifications to the manifested behaviours and individual histories of his patients. This resulted in a series of major categories and subcategories, with ever-increasing complexity.

This separation of types enabled Krafft-Ebbing to differentiate from other categories of homosexual those individuals whom we would now recognize as being transsexual. Krafft-Ebbing divided homosexuality into two major categories: acquired homosexuality and congenital homosexuality. Under both headings he described transgenderism. It is sometimes extremely difficult to understand how he distinguished between case histories which today would appear similar; perhaps this is because we no longer have the concept of acquired or congenital homosexuality. The cases Krafft-Ebbing presents are interesting, in that we see the subjects using the same ways of describing themselves as we see in case histories of transsexual people from the 1950s to the 1990s. For example, in Case 99 we see the first recorded usage of the term, 'I feel like a woman in a man's form' (*Psychopathia Sexualis* by R. von Krafft-Ebbing, London, F.R. Dancs and Co., 1893, p. 209), which became the classic phrase of self-description used by transsexual people in later years.

Magnus Hirschfeld (1868–1935) was the next most influential voice in sexology. Hirschfeld was both a doctor and a medico-legal expert in Germany's courts. He used his position to advance the science of sex to achieve social justice – for which he was hounded and his books burnt or pulped when the National Socialists came to power in 1933. Hirschfeld coined the word 'transvestite' from the title of his book *Die Transvestiten* published in 1910. It was Hirschfeld, in 1938, who finally separated transgendered behaviour from homosexuality, a separation that allowed the medical profession to take a specialized professional interest in the 'treatment' of the former.

Through the work of the early sexologists such as Krafft-Ebbing and Hirschfeld, transsexuality became a recognized phenomenon available for study, discussion and treatment. Throughout the 1930s and 1940s medical provision was very sparse but transsexual people still managed to find doctors who would help them.

Michael (Laura) Dillon managed to obtain gender reassignment treatment in the UK during the war. In the late 1940s he even had a 'penis' constructed by the plastic surgeon Sir Harold Gilles, who later became famous for his work with burns victims. Gilles developed the 'pedicle flap' which allowed skin tissue to be transported around the body whilst always maintaining a blood supply. This is still used as one of the main ways of creating a new penis. Michael Dillon trained and worked as a ship's doctor until he was 'outed' by the *Sunday Express* in 1958. He withdrew to India where he became a Buddhist monk and a writer on Buddhism, until his death in 1962.

Modern transsexuality

The first wave of publicity surrounding a transsexual person occured in 1953. Christine Jorgensen, a former American GI, returned from Denmark where she had undergone the first of several operations as part of her gender reassignment, and the news media picked up on the story. Overnight she became a news sensation and undoubtedly the most famous transsexual figure in the twentieth century. She was beautiful, blonde and everybody's idea of the 'all-American girl'.

Almost immediately her psychiatrist in Denmark, Dr Christian Hamburger, started receiving letters from people and in 1953 he published a paper entitled 'The desire for change of sex as shown by personal letters from 465 men and women' (*Acta Endocrinologica*, vol.

14, 1953, pp. 361–75). It was suddenly realized by medical professionals that these were not exceptional cases, but that there was a whole body of people who were desperately unhappy because their gender role did not match their body.

Christine Jorgensen, 1927–1989

Her very public life after her 1953 transition and surgery was a model for other transsexual(s) [people] for decades. She was a tireless lecturer on the subject of transsexuality, pleading for understanding from a public that all too often wanted to see transsexual(s) [people] as freaks or perverts. Although she considered herself primarily a photographer, she toured as a stage actress and singer. Ms. Jorgensen's poise, charm, and wit won the hearts of millions.

Candice Brown Elliot, 1999, http://www.transhistory.org

The endocrinologist Harry Benjamin (who had been on good terms with the sexologist Magnus Hirschfeld in Germany before the First World War) set up a clinical practice, firstly in New York and later in San Francisco. He started to train a new generation of psychiatrists and psychotherapists in the treatment of the transsexual person. One such therapist was Leah Schaefer, a former jazz and folk singer who, now in her 80s, still works with transsexual people in New York. In fact nearly all the major clinical provision for transsexual people in the world today has a direct lineage from Harry Benjamin, and therefore from Hirschfeld. The head of research at the major British Gender Identity Clinic at Charing Cross Hospital, Professor Richard Green, trained with Benjamin, as did Dr John Money who founded the first US Gender Identity Clinic at Johns Hopkins University Hospital in Baltimore. Most of the doctors now involved in arranging gender reassignment are members of the Harry Benjamin International Gender Dysphoria Association, which meets biennially and publishes the 'Standards of Care' that detail the medical and psychological provision and the manner of treatment with which transsexual people should be provided.

When Harry Benjamin published the first major textbook on the subject in 1966, gender reassignment was still the subject of extensive social stigma both publicly and in the medical world. (*The Transsexual Phenomenon* by H. Benjamin, New York, The Julian Press Inc., 1966) Over thirty years later some of that stigma remains but it is widely accepted that the only successful treatment for transsexual people is hormone therapy and surgical reassignment. A recent Appeal Court decision in the UK (NW Lancashire Area Health Authority v A, D and G, QBC 1999/0226/4, QBC 1999/0228/4, QBC 1999/0230/4, 1999) has confirmed this view, and gradually it is an area of medicine which is gaining respectability. Another factor contributing to this has been the widespread visibility of many more transsexual people. Wendy (Walter) Carlos is not just famous for her 'Switched on Bach' recordings, Jan (James) Morris the travel writer is not just famous for being the *Times* reporter on the 1953 expedition that conquered Everest, Billy (Dorothy) Tipton not just as one of the best jazz saxophonists of the 1950s. But these are just the tip of the iceberg, and many of us now know a colleague, a neighbour, a family member or just a friend of a friend. They have all made transsexuality a much more common feature of our landscape.

Transgender Issues

The 1960s – the beginnings of a movement

The transgendered (trans) community is a concept of the 1990s. Prior to the late twentieth century there is no evidence in Western culture of what might be called a transsexual or transvestite consciousness.

Early organization of the 'trans' community started through the work of Virginia Prince, an American cross-dresser and biological male who now defines herself as transgendered. In the 1960s she organized a network of support groups for transvestites, and published transvestite ephemera through 'Chevalier Publications'. In the late 1960s she became involved in a broad-reaching enterprise to educate the public about cross-dressing, transvestism and transsexualism.

From the small beginnings in the 1960s of a somewhat secretive network of social support groups, a huge system of self-help transvestite, transsexual and transgender groups has come into existence throughout the world. The 1980s saw a flourishing of publications such as support magazines coming out of these groups, and the 1990s has seen an extensive use of the Internet for support, personal exploration and, most significantly, politicization.

The Legal Situation in the UK

The UK remains one of only four out of 39 countries in the Council of Europe which fails to provide full legal recognition in their new gender for transsexual people: the others are Albania, Andorra and Ireland. This failure causes countless problems for transsexual people in their everyday lives. Despite being issued with corrected passports and driving licences reflecting their true gender, any situation requiring the production of a birth certificate guarantees a breach of personal privacy. The government insists that a birth certificate is not an identity document, yet civil service and public sector employers insist that it accompanies job applications.

Important to the understanding of the trans community's current ideas and thoughts on theories of gender are the transitions that their 'organizing centres' have gone through. From the self-help organizing of a few transvestite networks in the 1960s and 1970s, there is now a plethora of groups catering for representative diversity in cross-gender behaviour and lifestyles. Many people have been involved in the running of these groups for over a quarter of a century. They have an immense level of respect within their own community because of their strong commitment to, and knowledge of, the community and its history. Notwithstanding, many of them have also gone through great changes, personally and socially, both in their self-identification and in their public lives. This has not just been to do with aspects of their cross-dressing or transgendered behaviour, though that could be seen as being pivotal, but with their ongoing fight to get legal recognition, public respect and academic recognition for the work they have done in this area. Their personal roads to understanding gender and what it means have informed much of the current theoretical position, and the social activism which the trans community now undertakes.

Transgendered people have only very recently felt able to participate in academic discussions and social activism. There were several big obstacles to be overcome:

- the medical discourse surrounding transgendered behaviour which labels them mentally ill;
- social and legal restrictions which made it much easier to live a 'secret life';
- the feminist backlash originating with Janice Raymond's book *The Transsexual Empire, the making of the she-male* (London, The Women's Press, 1979);
- the view that transsexual people just conformed to sex stereotypes in their new gender role;
- the belief that transsexual people were simply repressed homosexuals.

In particular, much of the medical profession saw them as gay men or lesbians unable to 'hack it' as regards their sexuality and the law has refused to give full recognition of a gender role change. Also, many feminists still see transsexual people as misguided and mistaken men seeking surgery to fulfil some imaginary notion of femininity (FTMs do not exist in their world, except as misguided lesbians who betray their 'sisters') and the news media has fostered all these views by using transsexual people as the basis for sensational 'sex' stories.

Developing transgender theory

The 1971 case of Corbett v Corbett (Corbett v Corbett [1970] 2 All E.R. 33, 48; [1970] 2 W.L.R. 1306–1324), which involved the divorce of a transsexual woman, April Ashley, from her husband, was to lead to the current legal position of transsexual people. Judge Ormrod decided that a person's sex was defined through a three-part test: their chromosomes, gonads and genitals at birth. No allowance was to be given to psychological sex. Almost thirty years later Ormrod's decision is still good law in the UK, and as a result a transsexual person never changes sex.

New Zealand, most of the USA, Canada, Australia and many other countries have now rejected Judge Ormrod's ruling.

In the 1990s the trans community has tackled these issues head on. Firstly, they have challenged the medical profession's ability to diagnose transsexualism and they have argued that its primary role should be an enabling one, with supporting liaison psychiatric services to help deal with the consequences of stigmatization. Secondly, the trans community has consistently fought through the courts and the legislature for legal recognition of any new gender-role adopted and all that that entails, including the right to marry, adopt children, etc. They are also fighting for anti-discrimination legislation and policies to include not only sex and race, but also sexuality and gender identity.

The trans community has tackled radical feminist separatism by continually demanding answers to awkward questions about how we define sex and gender, and in particular challenging the right of any group to define others by their own limited view of the world.

> Along with male-to-female transsexuals, Leslie Feinberg, a 'female' transgenderist and author of *Stone Butch Blues* (Ithaca, New York, Firebrand Books, 1993), along with James Green, a transsexual man, contested the 'Womyn born Womyn' policy of the Michigan Womyn's Music Festival, by asking for their right (as born womyn) to enter the festival. Gradually the festival has changed its policies and instead allowed transsexual women to enter unchallenged.

The trans community has also been active in challenging heterosexism and patriarchy both within and without their own community. As to the issue of sexuality, through the work begun by Lou Sullivan (a gay transman who died of AIDS in 1991) and other gay, lesbian or bisexual activists, gay and lesbian transsexual people have come out. The argument is simple: if you can acknowledge in yourself that the body does not dictate the person, then you are in a privileged position to know that sexuality is a movable and mutable force within us all. In recent years, we have seen a proliferation of writing by members of the community. These are not just autobiographies and stories of 'sex changes', but also academic and political works which challenge the very knowledge the world holds about sex and gender, and the legal rights afforded through these categories.

Default assumptions are (as they always have been) one of the biggest problems facing the acceptance of the trans community's acceptance as who they say they are. There is the first assumption that females do not become men or males become women; instead they become pastiches, surgical constructions of imaginary masculinities or femininities. The default assumption is that gender is immutable, it is fixed through biological constraints, and social construction merely affects any representation that the biological may take. Trans activists and academics are attempting to deal with the volatile concept of identification, but it is against all odds; the rigidity of a set of default assumptions concerning sex-roles pervades all discussion of gender; the two have an incorruptible sameness that makes them all-pervasive. As Susan Segal said of the rest of the world: 'Challenge to our gendered "identities" may be more than we can handle.' (*Straight Sex: The politics of pleasure* by S. Segal, London, Virago, 1994.)

Yet gender and sex are fundamentally different to the trans community. They face the everyday reality of that difference in their lives, and attempts to reconcile it have led to unanticipated challenges. Many have had to move on from seeking the biological basis for their state of being since the search for a cause has been unsuccessful. Any aetiology that has been proposed, whether social or biological, has been torn down by the mass of exceptions. It has been accepted that seeking reasons is a fruitless occupation as the multiplicity of possible factors increases, and even if found and there were possible points of interception, the 'cure' might not be wanted.

Of great significance in the trans community has been the move away from the 'politics of passing'. 'Passing' – the achievement of feminine or masculine 'realness' – would provide for many a physically safe life, but it means living in constant fear of discovery. Furthermore, it means that all relationships begin as lies, and they rarely have a space in which the truth of one's journey across the gender divide could be told. In actual fact even the most 'passable' transsexual woman could find herself vulnerable; the model and 'Bond' girl Caroline Cossey (Tula) lost her privacy, employment and marriage after the *News of the World* published an exposé of her transsexual status in September 1982.

In the community in the past, those trans people who were the most 'non-transsexual' looking were awarded status and privilege, whilst those who were most obviously transsexual or transgender were often the butt of private jokes and exclusionary behaviour. But those who were most visible as trans were to be the people who daily faced the difficulties which often resulted in emotional, financial and even physical scars. The privileged few who 'passed' dictated for a long time which were the 'important' and 'significant' issues for the community. If you 'pass', because passing is about maintaining a secret in your life, then the important issues are seen to be those that would protect that secret, e.g. the right to have one's birth certificate reissued and the right to marry in one's new gender role.

But in reality, despite all that medical technology can achieve, the majority of trans women cannot and will never 'pass', and so a reissued birth certificate will certainly not prevent their discovery as trans, whether by prospective employers, observers on the street or a prospective marriage partner. Similarly for trans men, although 'passing' might appear at first glance easily achieved, the limitations of genital reassignment surgery mean that they will never be able to form a sexual relationship without having to disclose their past. In the 1990s the trans community took a serious look at itself and worked out that it was only by being inclusive of all trans people that the legal issues that caused real and universal oppression could be addressed. They had to develop a community voice that was truly representative of the real lives and the real problems they faced.

Crucial to the development of the new community voice was a response by trans academic Sandy Stone to Janice Raymond's 1979 anti-transsexual polemic *The Transsexual Empire, The Making of The She-Male*. In "The Empire Strikes Back, A Post-transsexual Manifesto" (in *Bodyguards: The Cultural Politics of Gender Ambiguity* edited by J. Epstein and K. Straub, London, Routledge, 1991), Stone says:

'For a transsexual, as a transsexual, to generate a true, effective and representational counter-discourse is to speak from outside the boundaries of gender, beyond the constructed oppositional nodes which have been pre-defined as the only positions from which discourse is possible.' (Stone, 1991: 295)

Sandy Stone had been an engineer at the all-women's record label, Olivia Records. She was attacked by Janice Raymond as a 'surgically constructed' representative of the patriarchy and a 'spy' who had invaded women's space. Raymond states:

'All transsexuals rape women's bodies by reducing the real female form to an artefact, appropriating this body for themselves ... Transsexuals merely cut off the most obvious means of invading women, so that they seem non-invasive.' (Raymond, 1979: 104)

The repercussions of Raymond's book are still being felt 20 years later, with many Rape Crisis Centres refusing to help transsexual women, and transsexual women being excluded from women's courses, women's centres and other women's spaces.

In her 1991 response, Stone called on all transsexual people 'to deconstruct the necessity for passing ... all transsexuals must take responsibility for *all* of their history.' (Stone 1991: 298)

She calls for transsexual people to claim their position as transsexuals and then to move beyond it and become post-transsexual – to gain a status beyond the medical category. As a result, the community terms transgender, and ultimately trans, have been developed to recognize the person, not just the medical status. Put simply, the community was called upon to be themselves and demand respect for themselves as they truly were.

Declaring a theory in which gender and sex roles are clearly separated (at least for a large number of people) and what that means to the modernist view of gender theory is a challenge the trans community is not ignoring. They are constantly querying their own sense of self and producing some very interesting answers which contest the very binary structure of the complacent world in which gender was invented, and by which it has become obsessed. To the trans community, gender has become a concept of the imagination that supports the very foundations of a patriarchal world in which anyone who expresses gender difference is oppressed.

The 1990s – the growth of transgender activism

After Sandy Stone's response to Raymond, one of the most significant pieces of writing to come out of the

Transsexual Menace is the most visible trans activist group in the USA. But in reality it is nothing more than a T-shirt. The distinctive black shirt simply states on the front: *The Transsexual Menace*. It is stylish, can be worn by anyone, trans or not, and is incredibly effective at getting the message across. Menace founder Riki Anne Wilchins is a transsexual woman who could choose to pass. She says that when she wears the shirt, the most significant thing it does is transfer the shame. Readers look at it, and then at her, and then at themselves as they realize that they are wondering and questioning, and that they don't know the answer. Most importantly they realize that it really should not matter what the answer is. For once they are more ashamed of what they are thinking, than the trans person is of themselves! The Menace tee shirt is now so popular that under the main logo there is a space in which the names of states can be added. There are now Menace tee shirts carrying the names of almost all the US states, UK, Sweden and Canada.

discovered simply because his documentation did not hide his past. Prior to the development of the trans community, Brandon Teena's death would have disappeared into a void. But local community trans activists picked up the news and within a short space of time, it was world news and reported extensively on the Internet in the magazines of numerous trans groups. Several vigils of support, organized by Transsexual Menace, took place with Brandon's family's approval. These were to culminate in a quiet vigil in Falls City, Nebraska, outside the Richardson County Courthouse, as the trial of John Lotter opened. Over forty transgender people travelled from all over the United States to participate. They had cooperative support from the local authorities, and extensive television coverage. Since then, local transgender groups have taken up the issues surrounding personal safety and many are involved in local campaigns for appropriate policing policies.

The past ten years have seen a huge rise in trans action throughout the world. Trans people are still campaigning for the basics; for gender reassignment itself in some countries. (The first legal gender reassignment surgery in Japan did not take place until 1998.)

Issues such as birth certificate changes and the right to marry have not been forgotten but these are contextualized within demands for respect and equality. Personal safety and anti-transphobia education programmes are high on the list of demands, along with workplace protection against discrimination and harassment, safety within housing and public spaces, equality of access to education and other social welfare provision, respect in medical care and the right to form families which have the same protections in law as other 'married' families have.

In 1996, the British lobby group Press For Change were to achieve a rare legal victory in the European Court of Justice (P v S and Cornwall County Council ECJ [1996] IRLR 347). The court held that it was illegal to discriminate against trans-sexual people in the workplace. This was the first decision in the world to afford workplace protection. The decision had effect throughout Europe, and has now been incorporated in British law (Sex Discrimination (Gender Reassignment) Regulations 1999).

Alongside this we have seen the steady rise of a trans culture, with artists such as Del LaGrace Volcano and Loren Cameron, writers such as Susan Stryker and musicians like Jayne County. This is a new community with a new sense of self-respect; it will not go quietly and it may well be that it changes the world for the better, for us all.

The Press For Change Agenda

Seven wishes that transsexual people have:

- Not to have to disclose details of our gender reassignment unnecessarily.
- To have the right to marry a member of the opposite gender, and to have all the benefits that accrue with marriage for ourselves and our partners – whether it is the right to claim a spousal exemption from inheritance tax, to claim a spousal pension, a right to jointly adopt children, or to make the claims that can be made upon separation or divorce.
- To have the right to retain a marriage celebrated before gender reassignment was undertaken.
- To have the freedom to enjoy a job without fear of dismissal or harassment because of our gender identity, our gender presentation or our gender role change.
- To have the right to use the legal process to protect ourselves in all aspects of our life in our new gender.
- To have the right to a social parental role, and to formalize it legally, in our new gender role.
- To have the right to be acknowledged at death as being a member of our new gender group, whether on registration of death, or in the consideration of wills, matters of intestacy, or inheritance.

Press For Change, founded in 1992, is the UK's lobbying and campaigning group for trans rights. It has the largest political campaign Web site of any lobby group, or political party, anywhere in the world and which receives over 40,000 hits each month, from all over the world. http://www.pfc.org.uk

Notable Episodes
in the History of a Movement

1910	Magnus Hirschfeld invents the term 'transvestite'.
1919	Magnus Hirschfeld establishes the Institute for Sexology in Berlin, Germany, the first clinic to provide regular counselling and treatment to trans people.
1931	First recorded 'sex change' operations take place in Germany.
1932	*Man into Woman*, the first autobiographical account of gender reassignment, is published.
1944	Sir Harold Gilles performs the first recorded phalloplasty, to create a penis, on a female-to-male transsexual.
1949	David Cauldwell coins the word 'transexual' (sic). Harry Benjamin opens clinics in New York and San Francisco.
1953	Massive publicity surrounds the return to the USA, from Denmark, of ex-GI Christine Jorgensen. Later the same year her doctor publishes details of letters he had received from over 460 other people who were seeking gender reassignment.
1954	Former World War II fighter pilot and racing car driver Roberta (nee Robert) Cowell publishes her autobiography and becomes famous as Britain's answer to Christine Jorgensen.

1966	Harry Benjamin publishes the first scholarly book on transsexuality: *The Transsexual Phenomenon*. The first gender identity clinic in the UK is set up at Charing Cross Hospital.
1968	John Money sets up the first gender identity clinic in the USA at the Johns Hopkins University Hospital, Baltimore.
1969	Police raid the Stonewall 'gay' Bar in New York. They attempt to arrest an FTM, who is dressed in leathers, for failing to wear three items of female clothing (at that time such a law existed in New York). Several trans women, including Silvia Rivera who was to found the first political trans group, STAR, along with several trans men fight back. The Stonewall Riots are the catalyst for the creation of the Gay Liberation movement.
1971	Transsexual woman, April Ashley, has her marriage declared void *ab initio* (i.e. it never existed) by the doctor and judge, L.J. Ormro. Ormro sets up the 'three congruent criteria' test for sex. These are that sex is determined on the basis of chromosomes, gonads and genitals at birth. As a result, in the UK post-operative transsexuals are unable to get their birth certificates amended or to marry. Sweden is the first country in the world to pass legislation recognizing the change in a person's legal gender.
1973	South Africa passes legislation to allow transsexual people to be legally recognized in their new gender role.
1974	Jan (née James) Morris, travel writer and *Times* journalist, publishes her autobiography *Conundrum* (London, Faber & Faber Ltd, 1974).
1976	Renee (née Richard) Richards is barred from a women's tennis tournament. Her subsequent legal battle establishes that transsexual people in the United States are able to be legally recognized in their gender role. The first British transsexual support groups are set up in London and Manchester.

1979	Janice Raymond publishes *The Transsexual Empire*, a radical feminist attack on transsexual people. The Harry Benjamin International Gender Dysphoria Association is founded to provide peer group support for all those involved in the care of transsexual people. The Association develops the Standards of Care. The Diagnostic and Statistical Manual of the American Psychiatric Association includes transsexualism as a distinct and separate diagnosis.
1984	Mark Rees takes the UK to the European Court of Human Rights. He is the first of many British citizens to seek recognition of their gender through the Court of Human Rights.
1989	Renowned jazz saxophonist Billy Tipton dies and is discovered to have been born female-bodied. His wife and children refuse to call him anything but a man and a father.
1991	Sandy Stone, transsexual woman and former engineer at Olivia Records, publishes *The Empire Strikes Back, A Posttranssexual Manifesto* which takes apart the feminist attack on trans people. It becomes the major influence in trans activism and the founding of the new school of trans theory.
1992	Press for Change is founded in the UK, to lobby and campaign for respect and equality for all trans people.
1993	American trans activists set up camp outside the Michigan Womyn's Music Festival to protest against the Festival's 'Womyn-Born-Womyn-Only' anti-transsexual policy. 'Camp Trans' is still being set up in 1999.
1994	The Gender Reassignment Bill is debated in the UK Parliament. It fails to be passed due to lack of time, but the word 'transsexual' is entered for the first time in the parliamentary record.

1996	P v S and Cornwall County Council is won in the European Court of Justice. It is the first decision in the world to afford transsexual people workplace protection. London's gay pride march includes 'Transgender' in its title.
1997	A petition of 10,000 signatures is presented to the UK government, asking for transsexual people to be legally recognized in their new gender role. First Transgender Film Festival in the world, held in London, followed a few months later by the second in San Francisco. Both are now regular features of the Arts calendar.
1998	Transsexual woman, Dana International, wins the Eurovision song contest for Israel. The Amsterdam Gay Games organizers insist on 'documented completion of sex change or two years of hormones' before allowing transgendered people to compete. Several trans people drop out of the Games in protest. Yet Dana International performs at the Games ceremony. South Africa includes protection for transsexual people in its constitution. Japan permits its first legal gender reassignment surgery to be carried out on an FTM. New South Wales, Australia, includes the word 'transgender' in its anti-hate crime laws and anti-discrimination laws.
1999	London's gay pride organizers drop 'transgender' from the march title. The UK government passes legislation to protect transsexual people in the workplace. The UK Ministry of Defence allows transsexual people to serve or continue serving in the armed forces. The UK government sets up a working group to look at transsexual people's issues; they are committed to reporting back by Easter 2000.

Glossary

Bi-gendered A person who feels that his/her gender identity includes both male and female elements.
Bi-lateral mastectomy The removal of some breast tissue from both breasts and the reconstruction of the chest wall to resemble a normal male chest.
Body image The internal perception of one's body, including not only what the body looks like, but feelings and sensations, the perception of one's own voice, and so on. Transsexuals usually have an internal body image that is at odds with their actual bodies, until this is altered via hormones and surgery.
Butch A certain sort of masculine appearance – as opposed to appearing male, often used to refer to 'butch lesbians/dykes' as opposed to femme dykes.
Cross-gender living Living in the gender role of the opposite anatomical sex group.
Drag king The art/performance of dressing up as male – rarely do drag kings identify as men, they identify as women who choose to dress up as men for certain social occasions. They are not trying to imply they are men.
Drag queen The art/performance of dressing up as female - rarely do drag queens identify as women, they identify as men who choose to dress up as women for

certain social occasions. They are not trying to imply they are women.

Endocrinology The field of medicine concerned with hormones, including the sex hormones: oestrogen and testosterone.

FTM Female-to-male, most commonly used to refer to a female-to-male transsexual or transgender person (transsexual or transgender man). However, the term is gaining usage in the lesbian community to mean women who have extremely masculine gender expression, including those who 'pass' as male yet still identify as female.

Gender An individual's personal sense of maleness or femaleness. It is also a social construction that allocates certain behaviours into male or female roles. These will not always be the same across history, across societies, across classes; hence we know that gender is not an entirely biological matter, rather it is influenced through society's expectations.

Gender dysphoria The term used by psychiatrists and psychologists to describe the condition transsexuals have – that is, not feeling well or happy with their gender as assigned at birth, in terms of both their social role and their body. Gender dysphoria is not characterized by denial; for instance, female-to-male transsexuals acknowledge that their (pre-transitional) bodies are female. The fact that their anatomy does not correspond with their sense of being male (psychological sex) leads them to seek to bring the two (body and mind) into harmony. Specifically, the diagnosis states that Gender dysphoria is 'characterized by a strong and persistent cross-gender identification' which 'does not arise from a desire to obtain the cultural advantages of being the other sex', and that it should not be confused with 'simple nonconformity to stereotypical sex role behaviour.'

The diagnosis is currently disputed by a number of groups, most notably gay and lesbian organizations (who protest the misuse of the diagnosis to eradicate cross-gender behaviour in children) and transgender organizations, whose members do not wish to have surgery (or view it as a choice rather than a necessity) and thus do not want to be 'stigmatized' by having a mental disorder. Many transsexual people wish for the disorder to be classified as physical rather than mental, especially in light of recent research showing the physical basis of transsexuality, but feel that until this occurs there needs to be a medical diagnosis to ensure the continued availability of treatment.

Gender identity A person's internal sense of being male or female. These senses of awareness affect the individual's conscious (and perhaps unconscious) cognitive processes, and in turn greatly influence his or her social interaction with others.

Gender Identity Disorder (GID) Listed in the Diagnostic and Statistical Manual of Mental Disorders (DSM-IV), and formerly called Transsexualism in the earlier DSM-III, this is the medical diagnosis by which most transsexual people in this country currently receive hormone therapy and surgery.

Gender role How a person expresses himself or herself in terms of traits commonly associated with masculinity and femininity. Gender role is largely a social construct, since every society has different ideas about what sort of dress or behaviour is 'appropriate' for males or females. However, children do appear to have an instinctive idea of male and female, and typically prefer to model their behaviour after that of the sex they identify with.

Genetic female/Real girl A woman who was born with female anatomy, as opposed to a woman who was born with male anatomy (a transsexual or transgender woman).

Genetic male/Bio boy A man who was born with male anatomy, as opposed to a man who was born with female anatomy (a transsexual or transgender man).

Hysterectomy The surgical removal of the womb and cervix.

Metoidioplasty (also called genitoplasty) The process whereby, when the clitoris has enlarged after testosterone hormone therapy, the clitoral hood is released, so enabling the clitoris to be more forward and upright and to resemble a micro-penis.

MTF Male-to-female, most commonly used to refer to a male-to-female transsexual or transgender person (transsexual or transgender woman).

Non-op A person who does not desire surgery, or does not need surgery to feel comfortable with his or her body.

Oopherectomy The surgical removal of the ovaries.

Orchidectomy The surgical removal of the testes.

Penectomy The surgical removal of the penile tissue – the precursor to the creation of a new vagina.

Phalloplasty The surgical creation of a 'penis-like' piece of flesh. However, a phalloplasty cannot create a penis – it is not erectile tissue, and it cannot have sexual sensation in itself. However, sometimes the urethra can be successfully extended through it so that urine may be passed standing, and sometimes implants can be placed in it so that penetration of a sexual partner can be achieved.

Pre-op/post-op transsexual Pre-operative and post-operative; having not had or had sex-confirmation surgeries. 'Pre-operative' implies that the person desires gender reassignment surgery; if this is not the case, 'non-op' is the correct term.

Scrotoplasty The surgical creation of an apparent scrotum.

SRS (sex reassignment surgery)/GRS (gender reassignment surgery) Medical term for what transsexual people often call gender-confirmation surgery: surgery to bring the primary and secondary sex characteristics of a transsexual's body into alignment with his or her internal self-perception.

Transgender An umbrella term used to define a political and social community which is inclusive of transsexual people, transgender people, cross-dressers (transvestites), and other groups of 'gender-variant' people such as drag queens and kings, butch lesbians, and 'mannish' or 'passing' women. 'Transgender' has also been used to refer to all persons who express gender in ways not traditionally associated with their sex. Similarly, it has also been used to refer to people who express gender in non-traditional ways, but continue to identify as the sex of birth.

Transgender person/Transgenderist As originally defined in the 1970s, a transgenderist is a person who internally identifies as the opposite sex, and lives as the opposite sex full-time, but does not feel the need to have surgery to change the body as transsexual people do. Sometimes also called a non-operative transsexual. Many transgenderists, however, do take cross-sex hormones. Some transgender people consider themselves a third sex, neither male nor female but combining characteristics of both (also called an epicene or 'third'). Most commonly, transgender people live as, identify as, and prefer to be treated as belonging to the 'opposite' sex, but do not wish to change their bodies through surgery.

Transition The process of beginning to live full-time as the opposite sex and changing the body, through hormones and surgery.

Transman A term used to denote both transsexual and transgender men.

Transsexual (female to male, male to female) A person who experiences a profound sense of incongruity between his/her psychological sex and his/her anatomical sex. Transsexual people wish to change the anatomical sex, through hormones or surgery, to match the internal perception of their bodies. There is increasing medical evidence, such as the recently published study from the Netherlands Institute for Brain Research, that transsexuality is an inborn condition that has its basis in the structure of the brain.

Transwoman A term used to denote both transsexual and transgender women.

Vaginectomy The surgical removal of the vagina and the closure of the vaginal opening.

Vaginoplasty The surgical creation of a vaginal opening and canal.

Further Reading

Blending Genders: Social Aspects of Cross Dressing and Sex-Changing by R. Ekins and D. King, London, Routledge, 1996.

Body Alchemy by L. Cameron, San Francisco, Cleis Press, 1996.

The Drag King Book by D. LaGrace Volcano and Judith 'Jack' Halberstam, London, Serpent's Tail, 1999.

FTM: Female to Male Transsexuals in Society by H. Devor, Bloomington and Indianapolis, Indiana University Press, 1997.

Gender Outlaw by K. Bornstein, London, Routledge, 1994.

GLQ: The Transgender Issue, Vol 4(2) edited by S. Stryker, 1998.

Journal of Gender Studies, Special Issue: Transgendering, Vol 7(3) by S. Whittle, 1998.

Lesbians Talk Transgender by Z. Nataf, London, Scarlet Press, 1997.

My Gender Workbook by K. Bornstein, London, Routledge, 1998.

Read My Lips: Sexual Subversion and the End of Gender by R. A. Wilchins, New York, Firebrand Books, 1997.

Reclaiming Genders: Transsexual Grammars at the Fin de Siecle by K. More and S. Whittle, London, Cassell, 1999.

Second Skins: The Body Narratives of Transsexuality by J. Prosser, New York, Columbia University Press, 1998.

Sex Changes: The Politics of Transgenderism by P. Califa, San Francisco, Cleis Press, 1997.